LOVING EVERY CHILD

Wisdom for Parents

The Words of Janusz Korczak

EDITED BY Sandra Joseph

FOREWORD BY Ari L. Goldman

ALGONQUIN BOOKS OF CHAPEL HILL   2007

*This book is dedicated to children everywhere,
especially Elle, Sky, and Luca.
Thank you for your gifts of love and laughter.*

Published by
ALGONQUIN BOOKS OF CHAPEL HILL
Post Office Box 2225
Chapel Hill, North Carolina 27515-2225

a division of
WORKMAN PUBLISHING
225 Varick Street
New York, New York 10014

First published in Great Britain by Thorsons,
an imprint of HarperCollins*Publishers,* in 1999 as *A Voice for the Child: The
Inspirational Words of Janusz Korczak.*
Printed in the United States.
Published simultaneously in Canada by Thomas Allen & Son Limited.
Design by Michael Fusco.

Translated by Theresa Prout and Anne Hargest Gorzelak.

Library of Congress Cataloging-in-Publication Data
Korczak, Janusz, 1878–1942.
[Voice for the child]
Loving every child : wisdom for parents / edited by Sandra Joseph.
p. cm.
Originally published: A voice for the child. London : Thorsons, 1999.
Quotations translated from the Polish.
ISBN-13: 978-1-56512-489-9; ISBN-10: 1-56512-489-8
1. Children. 2. Parent and child. 3. Children and adults. 4. Children's
rights. I. Joseph, Sandra. II. Title.
HQ767.9.K67 2005
305.23—dc22   2005050065

10 9 8 7 6 5 4 3 2 1
First Edition

CONTENTS

I was a very nervous new father. I didn't know how often to pick up my son, how hard to pat his back to burp him, or whether it was okay to let him cry. There were so many things. How do you know what to do?

My friend Lorraine, a wise woman who had raised many children and grandchildren, sensed my anxiety and, to calm me down, quoted Janusz Korczak. "Just listen to your son," Lorraine said. "He'll teach you how to be a father."

Two decades and three children later, I still marvel at that simple wisdom. Simply put, my kids taught me to be a father. All I had to do was listen.

"When is the proper time for a child to start walking?" Korczak asks in these pages. "When she does. When should her teeth start cutting? When they do. How many hours should a baby sleep? As long as she needs to."

Of course, Korczak realized that sometimes you need experts. He was not dismissing the advice of every doctor, writer, and educator. After all, he was all these things himself. But he believed that we as parents and as children have so much inherent knowledge; we must learn to trust ourselves.

"No book and no doctor is a substitute for one's own sensitive contemplation and careful observations," he writes. Books, he adds, can be of "small additional value," but no more.

I would add that in Korczak's estimation, the smaller the book, the greater the value.

The little volume you are holding in your hands can change your life as a parent. It can rescue you not only from "the experts" but also from over-medicating and over-evaluating and over-obsessing about your child. It might also help you strip away the earphones, the remotes, and the computers. What children really need is someone to listen to them.

How do you listen? I've struggled with this question both as a parent and as a journalist. Early in my career, I was an education reporter for a major American newspaper. I often went into schools to report. I'm pretty good at getting people to open up, but I could never get schoolchildren to talk to me.

Korczak had some good advice. "The child is small, light-weight, and there is just less of him," he writes. Imagine, he suggests, what we must look like to a small child. We're big; they're tiny. There's only one way to talk to them, he adds: "We ought to stoop and come down to his level."

Things changed for me when I got down on my knees. Once on their level, I found I didn't even have to ask questions. I just listened. If you're there listening, children will talk.

Children, of course, value little things far more than they value us. Korczak helps us gaze into their pockets and cubbies to see their treasures: pieces of string, nails, pebbles, beads, bits of colored glass, birds' feathers, pinecones, ribbons and bus tickets—as he puts it, "cherished belongings and dreams of a wonderful life." Later he adds: "Dogs, birds, butterflies, and flowers are equally close to his heart, and he feels kinship with each pebble and shell."

I shudder to think what Korczak would have thought of Game Boys.

Think about it. What would you rather find in your childrens' pockets?

Korczak died at the hands of the Nazis in 1942. Until his dying moments he comforted the two hundred orphans he cared for in the infamous Warsaw Ghetto. If you don't know the story of Korczak's brilliant career and tragic death, you can read it in the final pages of this book.

But what I particularly like about this volume is that it takes Korczak's wisdom about children out of the context of martyrdom. Most people learn about him through exhibits at various museums commemorating the Holocaust. Korczak, of course, deserves a place there. But he especially deserves to be remembered for what he taught us about children and about ourselves.

ARI L. GOLDMAN, a former reporter for the *New York Times,* is a professor at the Columbia University Graduate School of Journalism. He is the author of *The Search for God at Harvard* and other books.

INTRODUCTION

I hope that after reading this book the English-speaking world will finally become familiar with Janusz Korczak (pronounced *Korchok*) and his work. Most of the quotations are taken from *How to Love a Child* and *Respect for the Child,* books Korczak wrote over fifty years ago. But his insights and simple truths concerning children are as fresh and valuable today as they were then, for he was a man years ahead of his time.

By fate I fell into the world of Dr. Janusz Korczak while studying psychotherapy. Both Bruno Bettelheim and Alice Miller, two of the world's most famous child psychologists, had described Korczak as one of the greatest educators of all times and a true pedagogue. I tried to find out more about this man, especially his theories concerning education and child care. At libraries I came up empty. I asked teachers, social workers, therapists, and everyone I knew, but nobody had heard of him. Finally, by a strange set of coincidences, I was introduced to Felek Scharf, a Pole himself and an expert on Polish affairs, and one of the few living links to Korczak in the United Kingdom. Felek showed me two of Korczak's books that had been translated into English. One was the famous children's book *King Matt the First* and the other was *Ghetto Diary*.

"But what about his work on children?" I asked. Felek shook his head sadly. Very little had been published in English. I left with two treasured books by Janusz Korczak—*How to Love a Child* and *Respect for the Child*—but they were written in Polish. I felt so frustrated. Slowly, the idea dawned on me that these books must be translated into English.

Once the translations were complete, I was amazed by what I read. Korczak did not theorize, or give ready-made answers, but presented the fruits of his experience in such a clear simple way. Almost like that of a child, direct but at the same time poetic, so that every reader could not help but be inspired.

I have shown Korczak's writings to parents, teachers, social workers, and anyone whose life is involved with the world of children. However, it was the young people I have counseled over the years, many of whom had experienced abuse and neglect, whose reactions have surprised me the most: "If only my parents had read Korczak, they could have seen things from my point of view. Instead of feeling so isolated and misjudged, I could have quoted his words back to them. Maybe then they would have understood me." Korczak had always stressed the importance of "learning from the child" but, beyond that, he emphasized the importance of bestowing upon children the same rights we allocate to adults.

Korczak spoke of the need for a Declaration of Children's Rights, long before the one adopted by the League of Nations in 1924. In 1959, the United Nations produced its famous Universal Declaration of Human Rights, and not long afterward, a second Declaration on the Rights of the Child (November 20, 1959). This was a step forward for children's rights, but as a declaration this new set of principles was not legally binding and did not carry a procedure to ensure its implementation.

When the United Nations declared 1979 "The Year of the Child," it was also named "The Year of Janusz Korczak" to mark the centenary of his birth. Significantly, that same year Poland proposed a convention based on the teachings of Korczak, which would establish that all children shall be provided with education, social security, and health care; that they shall be protected from exploitation, abuse, torture, and the effects of war, and on reaching a reasonable age shall be consulted on any decisions involving them. The Convention on the Rights of the Child was passed unanimously by the United Nations General Assembly in 1989. It had taken the world over fifty years to hammer out the "rights" that Korczak had laid out in his books.

Korczak deserves to be recognized and honored today. He was a man of true compassion and humility who lived and died for his deep belief in and love for children. Korczak truly was the "Champion of the Child."

—SANDRA JOSEPH

No Book Is a Substitute

I WANT EVERYONE to understand that no book and no doctor is a substitute for one's own sensitive contemplation and careful observations. Books with their ready-made formulas have dulled our vision and slackened the mind. Living by other people's experiences, research, and opinions, we have lost our self-confidence and we fail to observe things for ourselves.

Parents find lessons not from books, but from inside themselves. Then every book they read can be considered to be of small additional value; and this one, too, will have fulfilled its given task if it has managed to contribute to bringing this idea home.

KNOW YOURSELF before you attempt to get to know children. Become aware of what you yourself are capable of before you attempt to outline the rights and responsibilities of children. First and foremost you must realize that you, too, are a child, whom you must first get to know, bring up, and educate.

A Child
Is Born

AS A MOTHER, YOU SAY: "My child."
When if not during your pregnancy do
you have more right to say this? The beat-
ing of the tiny heart, no bigger than a peach stone,
echoes your own pulse. Your breath provides the
child with oxygen. The blood courses through you
both and no drop of blood quite knows yet whether
it will remain the mother's or become the child's.
Every bite of bread becomes material for building
the child's legs on which she will run about, for the
skin which will cover her, for the eyes with which
she will see, for the brain in which thoughts will
burst, for the arms which she will stretch out and
the smile with which she will call you Mommy.

A S A PARENT, YOU SAY: "My child." No, the child belongs jointly to the mother, the father, the grandparents, and the great-grand-parents. Somebody's distant "I" which remained dormant in several ancestors, a voice emerging from a decayed, long-forgotten tomb, suddenly speaks again in this child.

A CHILD IS a piece of parchment which has been thoroughly covered with minute hieroglyphics, only a very small part of which will you ever be able to decipher.

A S A PARENT, YOU SAY: "She ought to . . . I want her to . . ." And you look for a pattern for your child to follow and you search for a life which you wish for her to have. You ignore the fact that all around you there is nothing but mediocrity and banality. People wander around, bustle, they fuss over small problems, fleeting aspirations, uninspired goals, unfulfilled hopes, perpetual longing.

Where is happiness? What exactly is it? Do you know the way to it? Are there those who might know? Will you be equal to the task? How can one anticipate the future and offer protection?

THE CHILD IS like a butterfly hovering above a raging torrent of life. How to imbue her with toughness without encumbering her lightness in flight; how to temper her without wetting her wings? Should one offer one's own example, help, advice, and words? But what if she rejects them all?

JUST REMEMBER: A child hungry for advice and direction will absorb it, digest it, and assimilate it. Overfed with moral rules the child will suffer from nausea.

AS A PARENT, YOU SAY: "Who is the child to become?" A warrior or just a worker, a leader or one of the followers? Or will she simply want to be happy?

A S A PARENT, YOU SAY: "She is supposed to be healthy, so why does she keep crying? Why is she so thin, why does she not suckle properly, why does she not sleep, why does she sleep so much, why does she have such a big head, why does she clench her fists, why is her skin so red, what about the spots on her nose, why does she squint, hiccup, sneeze, choke, sound hoarse? Is this normal?"

You look at this small, helpless thing, which does not resemble any of the other equally small and toothless creatures in the street or in the park. Can it be that in three, four months she, too, will become like them?

JUST REMEMBER: When is the proper time for a child to start walking? When she does. When should her teeth start cutting? When they do. How many hours should a baby sleep? As long as she needs to.

A S A PARENT, YOU SAY: "But is the child clever?" If a parent anxiously asks this question right from the start, it will not take long before the parent will be placing demands on the child. Eat up your food, even if you are not hungry and feel nauseated; go to bed, even though you are not tired and will have to wait an hour to fall asleep. Because you have to, and because I want you to be healthy.

JUST REMEMBER: Mentalities vary, and children can be steady or capricious, compliant or contrary, creative or imitative, witty or earnest, concrete or abstract; the memory can be exceptional or average; some are congenital despots while others have a wide range of interests.

How often do parents feel disappointment when children fail to live up to expectations, and how often do parents feel disappointment at every step of their development? Parents can be their harsh judges, rather than their counselors and consolers.

It is nothing but a mistake, utter foolishness, to imagine that everything which is not outstanding is therefore pointless and worthless. We are all suffering from the immortality syndrome. Anyone who has not managed to have a monument to himself erected in the marketplace would like a side street named after him at the very least, as a perpetual record.

As a parent, you say: "The child cries very little, she sleeps through the night." She is good-natured; she is a good child. A bad one is one who makes a fuss and a lot of noise and one who, for no apparent reason, evokes more unpleasant than pleasant emotions in her parents.

One must be careful not to confuse a good child with an easy one.

As a parent, you fully intend to look after all the child's needs, to bring her up rationally, in the modern way, under the supervision of an experienced doctor. Your child will have no reason to cry.

A painful surprise for every young parent is the noise the child produces. You have always been aware of the fact that children cry, but thinking about your own child you somehow overlooked this detail and expected nothing but charming smiles.

Is A NERVOUS child the way she is because her parents are nervous, or because of the way she was brought up by them? Where is the dividing line between the nervousness and a delicate nervous cast handed down by her spiritual ancestry?

Does a rakish father give birth to a profligate son, or does he infect him by example?

"Tell me who your parents are and I will tell you who you are."

But not always.

"Tell me who brought you up, and I will tell you who you are."

This is also not quite true.

WHEN A NEWBORN scratches herself with her own fingernail, when an infant puts her foot in her mouth while sitting up, or falls over and then angrily looks around for the person responsible for this, when she pulls her hair and grimacing with pain repeats the same experiment over again, when she knocks herself on the head with a spoon and looks up to see what struck her—the child does not know herself.

When she investigates the movement of her hand, when she carefully examines her fist while sucking away at it, or while toddling, she stops and looks down and tries to find something which seems to be carrying her along, when she compares her right foot inside a sock with the other one—she is trying to find things out and to understand.

When she tests the water in the bath and finds herself to be a conscious drop among all the other drops, it is then that she apprehends the important truth contained in the short word: "I."

HAVE YOU EVER watched an infant keep putting on and taking off a sock or shoe, for a long time, patiently, with a fixed expression, slightly open mouth, and total concentration? This is not a game nor imitation, and neither is it a senseless waste of time, but real work.

A child's development curve has its springtimes and its autumns, alternating periods of intense work and rest.

NOTHING SHORT OF a futurist painting could accurately depict a child's image of herself: fingers, fist, and less distinctly, the legs, perhaps the abdomen, maybe even the head, but in indefinite contours, like a map of the Arctic regions.

But this is not all, she is still turning around and bending over in order to see what is hidden behind her. She examines herself in front of the mirror and looks at her image in a photograph. And all this creates additional work for her, namely to find her place among her surroundings. There is Mommy, Daddy, and other people; some appear frequently, others more rarely.

And in the future, she will have to find her place in society, herself amid humanity, and herself within the universe.

Well, well, now the hair has turned gray, but this work is still not done.

Here and Now

APLEA ON BEHALF OF RESPECT FOR THE HERE AND NOW, FOR TODAY: How can we assure a child's life in the future, if we have not yet learned how to live consciously and responsibly in the present? Do not trample, hold in contempt, or sell the future into bondage. Do not stifle it, rush or force it. Respect every single moment, as it will pass and will never again be repeated.

After all, when tomorrow finally does arrive, we start waiting for the next tomorrow.

WHAT IS HE going to be when he grows up?" parents ask anxiously. They want their children to be better than them. Parents have a dream about a perfect man of the future.

Our indolence keeps us from discovering beauty in the present. What else if not a state of anticipatory hysteria do statements like the following signify: "If only he would start walking and talking at last?"

When I approach a child, I have two feelings: Affection for what he is today and respect for what he can become.

THE BASIC IDEA that the child is not now but will become later, does not know anything but will do so, is not capable of doing anything but will learn, makes us live in a perpetual state of expectation.

For the sake of tomorrow we fail to respect what amuses, saddens, amazes, angers, and interests him today. For the sake of tomorrow, we steal many years of his life.

When we say, "Children should be seen and not heard. You have all your life ahead of you. Wait till you grow up," the child is thinking: "I am nothing. Only grownups are worth something. I am getting a bit older, though. How many more years to wait? But just you wait till I grow up . . ."

WHY DO WE consider a child's spiritual entity different from our own? We put on it the burden of responsibilities belonging to a future man, but we do not bestow any of the rights of today's citizens on it.

Children make up a large proportion of humanity, of the population, the nation. They are our fellow citizens; they are our constant companions. They are here now, they always have been, and they always will be.

CHILDREN ARE NOT the people of tomorrow, but are people of today. They have a right to be taken seriously, and to be treated with tenderness and respect. They should be allowed to grow into whoever they were meant to be—the unknown person inside each of them is our hope for the future.

From the very earliest times, there is a feeling that anything big is more worthy than anything small.

"I am big," announces the child with glee, standing on top of a table. "I am taller than you," he proclaims with pride, comparing his height with that of a friend.

It is disagreeable to stand on tiptoe and not to be able to reach things, the little steps cannot keep up with the grown-ups' steps and somehow the tumbler keeps slipping out of the tiny hand. He finds it hard to grasp the doorknob, to look out of the window—everything seems to be too high up. No notice is taken of him in a crowd, his view is blocked and people keep bumping into him. No, all this is not very nice, and it is a nuisance to be small.

Everything that is big and takes up more room is respected and admired. Among things which impress everyone are big cities, high mountains, or a lofty tree.

The child is small, lightweight, and there is just less of him. We ought to stoop and come down to his level.

In Return

I S THE EARTH grateful to the sun for shining on it? Is the tree grateful to the seed that it grew out of? Does the nightingale sing to his mother thanking her that she used to keep him warm with her breast feathers? Do you make a gift to your child of everything which you have received from your parents, or do you only lend it to him in order to take it back again, writing everything down carefully and calculating the amount of interest due? Is love a favor for which you demand remuneration?

WE HAVE DRESSED children up in a uniform of childhood and we believe that they love, respect, and trust us, that they are innocent, gullible, and grateful. We are moved to tears at the thought of all the sacrifices we have made for their sake. As for their part, children get things from us by asking, by a charming smile, a kiss, a joke, by being obedient. They buy our favor by giving in to us. Occasionally, very tactfully, they let us know that they do have certain rights. Sometimes they force things out of us by harassment, other times they will ask openly, "What do I get in return?"

WE DISDAIN THE child because she does not understand the difficulties and complications of adult life. She does not know where our spells of excitement, discouragement, or boredom stem from, what sort of things destroy our peace of mind and put us in a bad mood; she is not aware of the setbacks and failures that adults suffer.

She imagines life to be simple and straightforward. There is Daddy and Mommy; they earn money and buy things. She doesn't know that human beings are engaged in a perpetual struggle to preserve what belongs to them and to acquire more possessions.

I should like to mention here the mutual love of parents. It is true the child seldom senses the lack of it when it is not there, but she does absorb it when it is.

Communication

A POET IS SOMEONE who is very happy and very sad, who is quick to anger and who loves intensely, who feels strongly. Children are like that, too.

A philosopher is someone who is very observant, who ponders and wants to know how things really are. Children are like that, too.

It is hard for children to say what they are feeling or what they are thinking about, because speech requires words. It is harder still for them to write, but children truly are philosophers and poets.

THE CHILD MUST be seen as a foreigner who does not speak our language and who is ignorant of the laws and customs. Occasionally he likes to go sightseeing on his own and when lost will ask for information and advice. Wanted—a guide to answer questions politely and patiently. Treat his ignorance with respect.

THE CHILD'S THINKING is neither more limited nor inferior to that of an adult. It is different. The child thinks with feelings and not with the intellect. That is why communication is so complicated and speaking with children is a difficult art.

THE CHILD IS HONEST. When he does not answer, he answers. For he doesn't want to lie and he cannot say the truth. Sometimes, silence is the highest expression of honesty.

THERE ARE MANY terrible things in this world, but the worst is when a child is afraid of his father, mother, or teacher. He fears them, instead of loving and trusting them.

If a child trusts you with his secret, be grateful. For his confidence is the highest prize.

IF A CHILD HAS a life where cruelty has become the norm, what a powerful effect would be the memory of that person—perhaps the only one—who showed kindness, understanding, and respect. The child's future life and sense of his self could take a different course, knowing there was one person who would not fail him.

A human being is responsible for his own spirit and his own thoughts, because these constitute his workshop.

The Right
to Be
Respected

A **PLEA FOR RESPECT:** Respect for the mysteries and the ups and downs of that difficult task of growing up. Respect for the here and now, for the present. How will she be able to get on in life tomorrow, if we are not allowing her to live a conscious, responsible life today? We must respect every moment, because each will pass and never return.

ADULTS OFTEN CAST a reluctant eye on the contents of a child's pockets and drawers. One can find almost everything there, including pictures, postcards, pieces of string, nails, pebbles, beads, bits of colored glass, stamps, birds' feathers, pinecones, ribbons, bus tickets, and leftover bits of things which no longer exist. Every little object has its history. These may be remembrances of things past, as well as longings for things to come:

A shell may represent a dream of a trip to the sea.

A screw and a few bits of wire—an airplane and dreams of flying.

A doll's eye, broken long ago—the only keepsake of a lost love.

Unfortunately, sometimes in anger or in a bad mood, the insensitive adult makes a heap out of these treasures and throws them away, because they are damaging pockets and jamming drawers. How heartless to treat other people's property in this way. How can one expect the child to have respect for anything or anyone? It is not bits of paper that end up in the dustbin, but cherished belongings and dreams of a wonderful life.

After many years in the field of teaching, it has become more and more obvious to me that children deserve respect, trust, and kindness. It is a pleasure to work with them in a cheerful atmosphere of merry laughter, lively first efforts, and pure, ebullient, affectionate joviality. The work is exciting, productive, and good.

A Child
Will Play

I T ISN'T WHAT the child plays that is important—it is how he plays and what he thinks and feels when he is playing that matters. A child can play intelligently with a doll and he can play a foolish game of chess. He can use a great deal of imagination and be totally absorbed in playing at being a policeman, a train driver, or a cowboy, and he can read superficially and without interest.

THE CHILD NEVER begrudges the time spent reading a story, having a conversation with the dog, playing catch, carefully scrutinizing a picture or retracing a letter. It is precisely the child who has got everything right, and we must give him freedom to drink his cup of happiness.

WHEN PLAYING, IT is not just that a child is in his element, but that this is the only range of activity where, to a greater or lesser extent, we allow him to take the initiative. While playing, the child is able to feel independent.

IS IT REALLY TRUE that a child does not enjoy work? The many games children play qualify as work. If four children decide to build a fort, using a piece of tin scrap, when they hammer in the nails, tie things up, put up a roof made of branches, lay a moss floor, working strenuously, this is not just play but work, albeit not very efficient, using imperfect tools and insufficient materials and therefore not as fruitful as it could be, but nevertheless organized in such a way that every one of them, regardless of age, strength, or level of competence, contributes as much effort as he is capable of.

I N A GAME SITUATION, small differences can always be observed. So let us to try to find out what the child's purpose in life is, and what he is able to give back in return. If we only ever see the child on his own, we will only have a narrow view of what he really is.

Observe the game in the garden: Who gives the signal, who organizes, who leads? Which children select their neighbors and which of them grasp any hands at random? Who is willing to let a new participant join in, and who protests against it? How many of them keep changing their positions and how many stay in the same place the whole time? Which of them wait patiently during the intervals and which are impatient, saying "Hurry up! Let's get started!" How many keep yawning but do not leave the game, and how many go off, either because they lose interest or because their feelings have been hurt? Which ones will keep insisting until they get one of the main parts?

A CHILD'S SUCCESS does not always depend on how adults judge him, but equally, and perhaps even in greater measure, on the opinion of other children: Let us see who can take bigger steps and how many steps with your eyes shut! Who can stand on one leg, not blink or laugh while staring into someone's eyes? Who can hold their breath for the longest time? Who can shout the loudest, spit the furthest?

CHILDREN CAN GET as drunk on the oxygen in the air as an adult on alcohol. The symptoms are excitement and recklessness, accompanied by embarrassment and sometimes a sensation of distaste and guilt. Even the most venerable individual may not be able to hold his drink.

One has no right to censure this; we should revere this happy drunkenness which occurs in children.

S OME GAMES CHILDREN play and the investigations and research they carry out are viewed with disfavor by adults. A child walks around on all fours and barks in order to find out how animals manage to do it; he may pretend to limp, or imitate a stooping old man, or he may squint, stammer, stagger like a drunk, imitate a madman in the street; he walks around with his eyes shut (blind), blocks up his ears (deaf), lies motionlessly holding his breath (dead), looks through a pair of spectacles, drags on a cigarette; he tears the wings off a fly to see how it will fly without them; he looks inside ears (what do these drums look like?), down a throat (what are these tonsils like?); he suggests playing doctor with a girl in the hope of having a look at what she has got inside her.

He wants to see and experience everything. In any case, so much remains which he will have to take on trust.

To what extent does the concept of possession tie up with the concept of power? Primitive man discovered that his bow and arrow were not merely a possession, but a hand which could strike at a distance.

Why Can't a Canary Go to Heaven?

BECAUSE A CHILD cannot be idle, she will poke into every corner, inspect every nook and cranny, find things and ask questions about them; everything seems interesting to her, the moving dot which turns out to be an ant, the glittering glass bead, or an expression which she may have overheard. Think how much we are like children when we find ourselves in a strange town or unusual surrounding.

A CHILD KNOWS his environment. She can sense kindness; she detects deceit. She is able to read a face in the same way a farmer reads the sky to forecast the weather. This is because she, too, has been observing and investigating things for many years; this activity is devoted to trying to fathom us.

A CHILD ALWAYS wants to know whether you have seen it yourself, or whether you found it out from other people, and where. She wants the answers to be brief and decisive, clear and honest.

A CHILD WANTS TO KNOW
ABOUT ANIMALS:

Bees have a queen, but why is there no king, is he dead? Why is it called a centipede when it does not really have a hundred legs, and, anyway, how many does it have then? Are all foxes cunning and is there no chance of them reforming and why are they the way they are? Does a dog remain faithful, even if he is being tormented and abused? And why are we not allowed to watch when one dog jumps on the back of another? Were stuffed animals once alive? Does a snail feel very uncomfortable and will it die if removed from its shell? Why is it so wet, is it perhaps a fish? Does it understand when we ask it to show its horns? Why do fishes have cold blood? Why does it not hurt when a snake changes its skin? What do ants talk about to each other? If you destroy a spider's web, will it die, or where is it going to find another piece of thread to make a new web? How can a chicken be born from an egg and do you have to bury the egg in the ground? How does a camel know how much water to drink to last him till the next time? So what is a dragon compared to all this? How could St. George kill a dragon if they do not exist? And if mermaids do not exist, why are there pictures of them?

A CHILD WANTS TO KNOW
ABOUT BODIES:

What happens inside the nose when you sneeze? Why can't I find out right now how children are born? Which is worse, to be blind or deaf? Why do children die and old people live on? Is one expected to cry harder when granny dies or when it happens to one's little brother? Why is it that a canary cannot go to heaven? When you dream something, is it for real, or does it only seem that way? What makes red hair? Which is worse, to eat a poisonous mushroom or to be bitten by a poisonous snake? Is it really true that if you stand out in the rain, you will grow faster? What is a shadow and why can't one run away from it? Is it also true that the teeth are covered with worms which cannot be seen?

A child wants to know about God:

Does a priest ever actually see God? Does God pray? What do angels do, do they sleep, eat, play ball, and who makes their dresses for them? Are the devils in terrible pain? Is it devils who poisoned the poisonous mushrooms? If God is angry with bank robbers, then why does he want us to pray for them? Why does Daddy not say his prayers, does he have God's permission not to? Is thunder a miracle? Is air God? Why can air not be seen? If it is not a miracle, why is it that no one knows how to make rain? What are clouds made of? Does the auntie who lives so far away live in a coffin?

A child wants to know about adults:

It is not nice to put your fingers in your mouth or to pick your nose. It is not nice to ask for things or to say, "I don't want to," or to move away when auntie tries to kiss you. It is not nice to yawn aloud or to say, "I am bored." It is bad to swing your legs, or to keep your hands in your pockets. It is not nice to make remarks in a loud voice or to point your finger. But why?

We plunder the mountains, cut down trees, and exterminate the animals. More and more the forests and marshes are being replaced by buildings. We are planting human beings in ever new territories.

We have subjugated the world and have made use of the iron and the animals; we have enslaved other races, we have organized international relations in a cursory way and appeased the masses. Injustice and ill treatment prevail.

We do not really consider childhood worries and apprehensions as very serious matters.

Any child is an unequivocal democrat and does not recognize any hierarchies. Whether it is another child's hunger or the agony of a tormented animal, it causes him pain. Dogs, birds, butterflies, and flowers are equally close to his heart, and he feels kinship with each pebble and shell. He does not believe that only humans have souls.

Adults Are Not Very Clever

A S ADULTS, WE don't like it when children criticize us. They're not permitted to notice our mistakes or absurdities. We appear before them in the garb of perfection. We play with children using marked cards; we win against the low cards of childhood with the aces of adulthood. Cheaters that we are, we shuffle the cards in such a way that we deal ourselves everything.

What children
really think of us:

ADULTS ARE NOT VERY CLEVER. They don't even know how to take advantage of the freedom they have. They're so lucky, they can buy anything they like, they're allowed to do anything they want, but despite all this they are always angry about something and any little thing is liable to make them shout.

❧

ADULTS DO NOT KNOW EVERYTHING. Sometimes, they answer just to get rid of you, or they make a joke. Sometimes, one will say one thing, someone else another, and it is impossible to tell who is telling the truth.

❧

THEY ARE NOT REALLY NICE. Parents feed their children, but they have to do it or else we would die. They don't allow children to do anything. They laugh when we say something, and then instead of trying to explain it to us, they tease us and make jokes about it.

THEY ARE UNFAIR. When they're in a good mood then everything is allowed, but when they're cross, every little thing disturbs them.

🌱

ADULTS LIE. It is a lie that one get sick from eating sweets, or that if you don't eat all your food, you will dream about monsters, or if you play with fire you will wet your bed, or if you swing your legs you are rocking the devil.

IN ADDITION TO the disdain which sometimes characterizes children's attitudes toward adults, one can also detect a certain amount of revulsion. A child finds a prickly beard, a rough face, and the smell of a cigar offensive. After every kiss, he wipes his face carefully, until he is told to stop. All these ladies and gentlemen who belch and suffer from flatulence, bad breath, who are tormented by a cough, have missing teeth, who find it difficult to walk upstairs, who have a bad complexion or a fat body, who wheeze—all this can be rather revolting in a child's mind.

It may be that the one positive feeling which children still manage to keep for us is pity.

ANY CHILD REALIZING my faults would be glad to change me, to make me better. The poor youngster cannot grasp the fact that my greatest fault is that I am no longer a child.

As adults, we often blame things on the fact that our upbringing was not what it should have been and now it is too late. Our faults and shortcomings have now become deep-rooted.

Is It Allowed?

A CHILD ASKS: Is it allowed? Adults do not allow it because it is bad for you, because you're too small, or it's just not allowed, and that's the end of it. But even here things are ambiguous. Some things are bad for you if Mommy happens to be angry, but sometimes even a little child is allowed it, especially if Dad is in a good mood or in front of visitors.

A S A PARENT, YOU SAY: "Don't run about or you will get run over. Don't run about or you will get too hot. Don't run about or you will get dirty. Don't run about, I have a headache."

But, in principle, we do allow children to run about—it seems that this is the only activity where we still allow them to show a sign that they are alive.

So DOES THIS MEAN that everything should be allowed? Never, not on your life. By prohibiting things, we are coaxing the will in the direction of self-control and self-denial. We also encourage inventiveness so a child can operate within a limited sphere. It gives her the ability to escape supervision. When we allow "everything," we must be careful.

The child's "give me," or even simply her silently outstretched hand, must learn to take our "no" for an answer. On this early "you can't have it, you shouldn't, you mustn't," an enormous part of her education depends.

How do you hope to initiate your child into life, if she holds the conviction that everything is correct, just and rationally motivated and consistent? Teach children not only to value truth, but also to recognize lies; not only to respect, but also to feel contempt; not only to become reconciled, but also to feel outrage; not only to give in, but also to rebel.

I believe many children rebel against virtue because they have been incessantly trained and overfed in its vocabulary. Let the child discover for herself, slowly, the need for altruism, its beauty, and its sweetness.

DO ALLOW CHILDREN to make mistakes and to joy-fully strive for improvement. Children love laughter, running about and playing tricks. If your own life is like a graveyard to you, leave children free to see it as a pasture.

If you witness a child's happiness in all its intensity, then you cannot fail to notice that the highest level of joy results from having overcome some obstacle—from a goal attained or a mystery solved. This is the happiness of triumph and the bliss of independence.

The Soul
of a
Child

THE SOUL OF A CHILD is as complicated as ours and is as full of contradictions. A teacher who, instead of forcing, emancipates, who does not pull but raises up, does not oppress but molds, does not dictate but instructs, does not demand but asks, is destined to live through many inspired moments together with the child and will frequently be able to observe, through a veil of tears, the struggle between good and evil forces and to watch the white angel walk off with the trump card.

I ASK YOU, WHY is it that a child, having overheard a curse, wants to keep repeating it, in spite of it being banned? Why does the child put up resistance when he could just as easily give in?

Or maybe the child has told a lie. He has secretly scraped the jam out from the inside of the cake. He has lifted up a girl's dress. He threw stones at frogs. He laughed at a fat man. He broke a china figure and put it back together so no one would notice. He smoked a cigarette. He was angry and he cursed his father in his thoughts.

When the child has done something wrong, he realizes that it is not for the last time, and that something is bound to tempt him to do it again or someone will talk him into it.

JUST REMEMBER: It's a sad moment when the child realizes that he is different and difficult. He looks for help, if he has enough courage to trust someone. He will seek refuge and ask, "Can you save me?" He confides his secret. He wants to be better.

A CHILD CAN BE dreadfully lonely in his suffering. Alongside the few children who live in a state of joy and revelry, whose lives are like a fairy tale, there are many to whom, right from their earliest youth, the world makes known the gloomy facts of life in plain, harsh phrases.

JUST REMEMBER: The child is influenced by what he sees and hears at home, in the school hall, in the yard, or on the street. He speaks in the language of his environment and imitates its gestures and follows its examples. We are never likely to meet a completely pure child—every one of them is tainted, to a greater or lesser extent.

THE CHILD OFTEN attracts our attention only when he disrupts or disturbs us and we remember only those instances. We do not notice him in his quiet, serious, and concentrated moods. We ignore the mystical moments when he converses with himself, with the world, and with God.

I never realized that a child is capable of remembering so well and of waiting so patiently.

Adolescence

A S AN ADOLESCENT, the child knows certain things. She knows that everything is not right with the world, that good and evil, knowledge and ignorance, justice and injustice, and freedom and dependence exist side by side. She does not understand everything—this is not really the point, after all—but she comes to terms with it all and decides to swim with the tide.

THIS STAGE OF MATURATION could be described something like this: I know all about it, but I don't feel anything yet; I can sense it coming, but I don't quite believe it.

S HE GROWS AND GROWS. Days and nights, asleep or awake, happy or sad, mischievous or contrite, she grows and grows. One day she needs to run, she feels like wrestling, conquering; another time she would rather hide away and dream and give herself over to melancholy. One day she may desire something passionately and the next day feel quite disheartened.

We should have more respect for the mysteries and fluctuations of the hard business of growing up!

WE DON'T LIKE IT when a child who has just been scolded keeps mumbling something under her breath because in her anger, she might let slip what she really thinks of us, which we may not be too keen to hear.

But how are we going to accept sulking, anger, and sarcasm as well?

AT THIS ADOLESCENT stage, the epidemic of whispered secrets accompanied by fits of giggling starts to die down, and the child begins to have earnest shared confidences. Friendships become deeper.

A BOY MAY LOVE a girl because she is not as silly as all the others and she is so jolly and she does not quarrel, because she wears her hair loose, because she is just very nice. She may love him back because he is not like the other boys, he is not rough, because he is so funny, because his eyes shine, because she likes his name, because he is just very nice.

LOVE IS INVARIABLY suspect and ridiculous. So we laugh when a six-year-old gives a little girl half of his piece of cake; we laugh when a little girl turns crimson when a schoolboy waves to her in the street. We laugh when we catch the schoolboy staring at her photograph; we laugh when a girl leaps up to open the door for her brother's tutor. But we frown when the two of them seem to be playing a bit too quietly together, or when they fall breathless to the ground after a wrestling bout.

WHAT IS IT THAT drives young people into a life of artistic Bohemia? Some are driven by the promise of fast living, others by its exotic aspect, another by sheer whimsy, ambition, and dreams of fame. But who teaches young people which compromises are necessary in life, which can be avoided, and, if so, at what price?

LIFE ITSELF IS NOT enough, so dreams become an escape from it. Feelings which have no other outlet flow into dreams. A dream is a program for life. If only we knew how to decipher them.

AN ADOLESCENT CHILD SAYS: Oh, to be grown up at last, to get away from this "transitional" age! It's time for fame, heroic deeds, travel, change of scenery, and experiences. It's time for dancing, fun, the sea and the mountains!

Politicians and legislators make rules and decisions about children, which often fail to work. But who asks the child for his opinion or consent? Who is likely to take note of any advice or approval from such a naive being? What can a child possibly have to say!

A Child
Brings

ACHILD BRINGS A marvelous poetic silence into our lives. The contentment of our lives depends on the many hours that we spend alongside our children, when they are not demanding attention but are just living.

We really do love our children. After all, in spite of everything, they are the comfort, cheer and hope, happiness, repose, and glowing radiance of our lives.

I HAVE THE MIND of a researcher, not an inventor.

To study in order to know? No.

To study in order to know more? No.

I think it is to study in order to ask more and more questions.

We all are brothers and sisters,
children of the same earth.
We have been preceded by
generations that shared a common destiny for good
and evil—one long common path. We get light
from the same sun and our crops are destroyed by
the same hail. The same earth covers the bones of
our forefathers. We have known more sorrow than
joy, more tears than laughter, and neither you nor
we bear the blame for this. Let us all work together,
let us educate ourselves together.

Who Was This Man?

I am not here to be loved and admired,
But to act and love.
It is not the duty of people to help me,
But it is my duty to look after the world,
And the people in it.

—JANUSZ KORCZAK

ORN HENRYK GOLDSZMIT in Warsaw on July 22, 1878, Korczak was the descendant of two generations of educated Jews who had broken away from Jewish tradition to assimilate themselves into Polish culture. His grandfather was a highly regarded physician, his father an equally successful lawyer. His early life appeared happy and sheltered, but was shattered at the age of eleven when his father suffered a mental breakdown and had to be institutionalized. Korczak was eighteen when his father died. Most of the family's savings had been spent on the high fees of the mental institution, and they had no financial means left. They were forced to move from their affluent quarters to a poor district of Warsaw. The next few years proved difficult ones for Korczak, who became the sole breadwinner for his mother, grandmother, and sister. After studying all day at high school, he would give private lessons to students who needed the extra help. At night he wrote short stories, satires, and poems, selling them to a literary weekly newspaper and various other periodicals.

When he was twenty years old, he was awarded first prize in the Paderewsky literary competition, one of the most prestigious in Poland. On the last day for entering the competition, he realized that he had not devised a pseudonym as required in the rules. Upon opening a historical novel by his side, he took the name of its hero, Janasz Korczak. A typesetter mistakenly changed "Janasz" to "Janusz" and so it remained.

It was not by chance that Korczak, torn between writing and medicine as a career, chose the latter. He wanted to help people, especially the sick and the poor. As he said, "Writing is only words. Medicine is deeds." However, Korczak managed to successfully merge both these activities. As a medical student at Warsaw University, he moved to a district of Warsaw stricken by poverty and illiteracy, where in his spare time he taught children and helped the disadvantaged in any way he could. His first book, *Street Children,* gave a realistic description of his experience of life in the slums and increased his popularity as a writer. He became involved in the Polish socialist parties, but what he learned of their political activity led him to withdraw. He believed in socialism, but only to the extent that it attempted to rectify social injustices. He formed the maxim: "If you want to reform the world, you must reform education." When Korczak eventually qualified as a doctor in 1904, he decided to specialize in pediatrics, and started work in the Warsaw children's hospital.

One year later, Korczak was enlisted as a doctor by the Russian Army during the Russo-Japanese War. During his service at the front, where he witnessed the full sufferings and injustices of war, he wrote: "War is an abomination. Especially because no one reports how many children are hungry, ill treated, and left without protection. Before a nation goes to war it should stop to think of the innocent children who will be injured, killed, or orphaned. No cause, no war is worth depriving children of their natural right to happiness. One must think first of the child before making revolutions."

After the war, Korczak traveled to Berlin, Paris, and London to further his medical studies. Upon his return to Poland, in order to gain a deeper insight into the field of child psychology and behavior, he accepted the position of supervisor and educator at the Company of Children's Camps, which organized summer holidays for the underprivileged children of Warsaw. Korczak's experience in these camps influenced him greatly and led him to devote more and more time to the care and education of children.

Meanwhile, his professional reputation among medical students and educators had been growing rapidly. Admirers came from far and wide to attend his lectures. He was constantly sought after as a physician to the wealthiest families in Warsaw, but at the same time he always accepted the "undesirable" house calls that other physicians refused. Though his professional fees were high for his wealthy patients, he treated poor families free of charge, often leaving money to pay for a prescription.

In 1912, while in his early thirties, the educator in Korczak emerged. Merely taking care of sick children no longer satisfied him; he had seen how helpless medicine was in dealing with social factors. As he put it, "A spoon of castor oil is no cure for poverty and parentlessness." He accepted the position as director of a new Jewish orphanage, whose well-equipped building, considered one of the most beautiful and advanced in Europe, he personally designed and planned. From then until his death he worked in the orphanage, living in the attic and receiving no salary.

Drawings in this chapter are by ITZHAK BELFER, who was born in Poland in 1923 and was brought up in Janusz Korczak's orphanage in Warsaw. When Warsaw fell to the Germans, Belfer escaped through the Polish forests to Russia. In 1947, sailing to Israel as an illegal immigrant, he was captured by the British and interned in Cyprus, where he began painting the desolate winter prison camps. Since 1948 he has lived in Israel, teaching art. His work has been exhibited worldwide.

The only interruption came when he served for four years as a doctor in the Russian Army during the First World War. It was in the midst of all this bloodshed, at stops on the road while treating wounded and dying soldiers, that Korczak wrote his most important work, *How to Love a Child*. In it he combined his experiences and observations concerning the spiritual and practical nurturing of children. The book became a vehicle with which to enter a child's mind.

The period between the wars, from 1918 to 1939, was fruitful for Korczak. And for the children in his care, the orphanage was an island of happiness compared to others that existed in Poland at that time. Nowhere else were such advanced educational theories and methods being practiced. He was no starry-eyed idealist: his insights into children were unclouded by sentimentality, for they were based on continuous clinical observation and meticulous listing of data. Wise, loving, and utterly single-minded, without a thought for such needs as money, fame, home, or family, Korczak was endowed with an uncanny empathy for children and a deep concern for their rights.

In 1922, together with Maryna Falska, a Polish social worker, he set up a new orphanage, this one for Catholic children. In both places he employed the same methods and enjoyed the help of dedicated assistants. Chief among them was Stefania Wilczynska, who worked at his side for over thirty years. Korczak was like a father to the children, constantly busy, disappearing

and returning, while Stefania was a mother—the permanent presence. The two became the perfect team, with Korczak's creativity and imagination complemented by Wilczynska's practical abilities.

Always, Korczak continued to write. In 1923 he published his children's book, *King Matt the First*, which was and is as famous in Poland as *Alice in Wonderland* and *Peter Pan* are here, and which has now been translated into over twenty languages. The story follows a little prince who inherits the crown of a kingdom and battles against all the injustices of the world, especially those inflicted on children by adults. It is a rare masterpiece of insight into how a child views the world of adults.

AGAIN AND AGAIN, Korczak stressed the importance of respecting and listening to children. Both in theory and in practice Korczak was always careful to refrain from any overuse of his power as an adult. He believed good educators should always seek to improve and instruct themselves in their work, and that adults could learn the most by allowing the children to teach them.

Within the orphanage he put his beliefs into practice by creating a Children's Court presided over by five child judges. The clerk of the court was a teacher. Every child with a grievance had the right to summon the offender to face the court of his peers. Teachers and children were equal before the court—even Korczak had to submit to its judgment. During one six-month period, Korczak found himself accused six times. He envisaged that within fifty years every school would have its own court and that it would become a source of liberation for the child, teaching both respect for the law and individual rights.

One of Korczak's most original innovations was the founding of a popular weekly newspaper called the *Little Review,* which he started in 1926 and which was produced for and by children. Mailboxes were set up across the country for children to submit questions and problems. "There will be twelve telephones," he wrote in the prospectus, "so that anyone can talk, ask questions, or make a complaint at whatever time they want. There will be three editors—one oldster—bald and bespectacled—and two additional editors, a boy and a girl." The editors, reporters, and contributors all received a small salary for their work. Korczak himself rarely wrote for the paper, but every Thursday he presided over a weekly meeting of the newspaper's correspondents. The *Little Review* continued publication until the outbreak of war in 1939.

During the interwar period, anti-Semitism began to increase in Poland, coming over in waves from Germany. Korczak, despite his reputation, was not immune to it. In 1935 he was engaged as "The Old Doctor" on the Polish state radio to give talks and answer questions on the subject of children and child care. The radio station heads, who held him in high esteem, didn't dare divulge his real name because he was a Jew. In a short time, his warm, friendly voice, along with his natural humor, won him a huge audience all over Poland. The editor of the Polish radio magazine *Antena* described Korczak's broadcasts: "He talked to children, but adults were also mesmerized. The

'Old Doctor' emphasized that only love could tie both young and adult man with the world. He was the greatest intellectual and humanist on the Polish radio. He talked with us humbly, quietly, caringly, and hesitatingly. He would look at us, watching our suffering, our pain, our poverty, and doubts. Seeing and understanding us, but still examining, holding his stethoscope to the heart and the soul and then carefully giving his diagnosis."

As political conditions deteriorated, Korczak decided to visit Palestine, where some of his former orphans had settled. The profascist right in Poland was on the ascendance, and vigilante groups and anti-Jewish riots had already appeared on the streets. Korczak sensed that the Jews of Poland were sitting on a tinderbox. Wilczynska was already in Palestine. Having traveled there in 1932 to visit a friend, she had decided to stay longer and was now working in a children's home on a kibbutz. Wilczynska was full of admiration for the commune's educational system and urged Korczak to come and see for himself. Her letters to him awakened his interest and curiosity. He went to Palestine in the summer of 1934 and stayed six weeks.

On September 1, 1939, the Germans invaded Poland.

Korczak knew the end was coming. A year later the Nazis ordered the Jewish orphanage on Krochmalna Street to relocate in the ghetto, along with the rest of Warsaw's Jews. Conditions within the ghetto were deplorable. Starvation and disease were rampant, and the bodies of the dead and dying on the streets became a common sight. Obsessed by a sense of personal responsibility for the survival of his children, even though he was ill and starving himself, Korczak became a "beggar for the most helpless." With a sack thrown over his back, he made his daily rounds seeking food and medicine for his charges. Committed as he was to the impossible task of caring and providing for his children, Korczak also undertook another mission. He agreed to take over what was known as the Orphans' Refuge, used as a temporary hospital for dying and sick children. Here, he spent all the time he could spare tending to the dying. He arranged for makeshift bunks to be built, so that the children could die with dignity.

While hunger was growing and disease spreading, Korczak tried to maintain some pretense of normalcy in the orphanage—teaching, playing, and caring for the children. His devoted friends and followers on the Aryan side made countless attempts to persuade him to save his own life, but his reply was always the same: "You wouldn't abandon your own child in sickness, misfortune, or danger, would you? So how can I leave two hundred children now!"

His growing sense of despair made him anxious to leave a final testament, which he did in his *Ghetto Diary*. On the last pages he wrote: "I am angry with nobody. I do not wish anybody evil. I am unable to do so. I do not know how one can do it." Korczak lived according to what the rabbinical fathers once wrote: "When asked 'When everyone acts inhuman, what should a man do?' their reply was 'He should act more human.'" This is what Korczak did to the very end.

The description of the death march of Korczak and his children on August 5, 1942, has become legendary. Weakened by fatigue and undernourished, Korczak walked with his head held high, leading his two hundred children in calm, orderly ranks through the hushed streets of Warsaw to the train station. They carried the orphanage flag that Korczak had designed—green with white blossoms on one side and the blue Star of David on the other. As one eyewitness recalled: "I will never forget that sight to the end of my life. It was a silent but organized protest

against the murderers, a march like which no human eye had ever seen before. It was an unbearably hot day. The children went four by four. Korczak went first with his head held high leading a child with each hand. The second group was led by Stefa. [Wilczynska had returned from Palestine in 1939 when she realized that war was inevitable; she said that she would be more useful helping in the orphanage than she would be in the kibbutz.]

They went to their death with a look full of contempt for their assassins. When the ghetto policemen saw Korczak they snapped to attention and saluted. 'Who is that man?' asked the German soldiers. I hid the flood of tears that ran down my cheeks with my hands. I sobbed and sobbed at our helplessness in the face of such murder."

Without a backward glance, Korczak, Wilczynska, and the other teachers helped the children, each carrying a favorite toy or book, up onto the ramps of the waiting freight cars whose final destination would be the gas chambers of Treblinka.

The famous Polish writer and journalist Marek Jaworski wrote: "The bodies of Janusz Korczak and his children were burned. All that is left of them is a handful of ashes and clouds of smoke, which the wind has scattered to the four corners of the earth. However, with this smoke Korczak's ideas circulate around the world—ideas which nothing can destroy or consign to oblivion now."